The Classical Couponer

*What hath Aristotle to do with the Kroger®
Mega Sale?*

~A busy mom's guide to 21st century
couponing

By Erin C. Lichnovsky

Special Thanks

To Joey – you are my continual fountain of inspiration and love, thank you for your undying devotion to marriage and family. Your unconditional love and acceptance is transformational.
I will forever and always love you.

To my children: Bethany Grace, Cameron True, Cassidy Joy, Benjamin Cole, Abigail Rose, Alacrity Hope, Charis Faith, and Adaya Mercy – You bring beauty and meaning to my life, and you make me want to be a better mom.

To the CallMOMs: Johnnie Seago, Rachelle Davis, and Terri Bonin – thank you for being godly examples of strong and courageous women of faith, fearless writers who speak truth to the culture, and courageous mothers who stand their post with an immovable conviction.

To the Lord Jesus – For it is in YOU I live, and move, and have my being.

"Our people must learn to devote themselves to doing what is good, in order that they may provide for daily necessities and not live unproductive lives." **Titus 3:14**

We believe God is going to do mighty things with this book. Not just because you give the ins and outs of coupon shopping, but because you live the life of a frugal woman. Your passion is to serve God by not being a slave to debt and over spending. You not only have a lot of experience and guidance on this subject, you live it every day. You can model how being good stewards with whatever money God gives us is serving our husbands as well as our God. Your ministry is SO big in this area. We have watched you inspire the wealthy, the poor, the young, the old, the newly married and the long time married with your commitment to saving money. You are the Moses for this project. We are, humbly and gratefully, your Aaron's.

~ The CallMOMs ***www.callmom.co***

The Classical Couponer
What hath Aristotle to do with a Kroger Mega Sale?

A busy mom's guide to 21st century couponing

"Educating the mind without educating the heart is no education at all"
~Aristotle

You might ask, "What IS a Classical Couponer? Isn't couponing a modern day phenomenon? And what on earth does it have to do with anything from the Classical era of *Aristotle*? Are there transcendental values inherent in the life of a coupon mom? And most importantly….what does it mean to me?"

If you are reading this book, you are most likely looking for one thing and one thing only - a way to make MONEY by cutting down on your grocery bill, *without* becoming the crazy coupon lady who has 5000 rolls of toilet paper in her basement and 1000 Butterfinger bars in her kid's dresser drawers.

How can we, as mothers, live a life of truth, beauty, and goodness while we are overwhelmed with sale ads, internet sites, Sunday papers, and expired coupons? It is my hope and desire to show you that you can live that life: with a simple, balanced, and systematic approach.

In ten easy steps you will learn: How to begin simply and finish strong, what to do first, setting up and organizing your system, the art of timing the sales, which internet sites can help you win at couponing, and much more.

My personal couponing journey may or may not be like yours, but through much encouragement from friends and family, I would like to share my experiences with you and show you that:

- ✓ There is a proven, tried-and-true system, to saving money that will work EVERY TIME.
- ✓ When store coupon policies constantly change, TV show-extreme-coupon- junkies clear the shelves, and new apps come out so fast that even your teenager can't keep up.....*you can still win at this.*
- ✓ Stockpiling is not a vice, but hoarding is.
- ✓ Busy, modern day moms *can* do this.
- ✓ Couponing can provide a way for your family and community to give out of your abundance.
- ✓ The transcendental values of truth, goodness, beauty, and love really can exist in the life of a couponing mom.

What is *your* goal? Save money? Pay off debt? Build a resource for ministry and giving? Teach your children to be good economists? Be a good economist yourself? If you said yes to any or all of these you can begin here....Let's lock arms together and let this wonderful journey begin!

A Personal Note:

Busy for me looks like this: I am a stay-at-home mom of eight children ages 19 to 13 months all living at home. We have been home-educating for the past 14 years and my husband also works from home. All ten of us live happily in a three-bedroom, two-bath home in Magnolia, Texas.

Over the years we have participated in outside classes, church activities, sports, theatre, music lessons, voice lessons, family nights, co-ops, and education programs. No, I don't do all these things every season, but we do participate weekly in a full and active schedule. Due to tight budget constraints, we drive used cars, wear hand-me-down clothing, and cook almost every meal at home. "Busy" defines our status quo.

A few years back, I was earnestly praying for my husband and our family finances. There never seemed to be enough money left at the end of the month and I knew how hard he was working and how stressful it was for him. After all the years of staying home with the kids I was seriously talking to my husband about me getting a part-time job to help us make ends meet. When I took a hard look at our family spending habits, I was shocked to see our food budget well exceeded our mortgage by almost 50% ! I began looking for a better way to feed our growing family on less.

One December, I stumbled onto a couponing site, and decided that I was going to "hire myself" and figure out how all these women were saving thousands of dollars a year with coupons. Being the right-brain learner that I am, pictures were what motivated me. I began to search through the coupon site message boards for "stockpiling images"….and that was all it took!

Looking at other people's pantry stockpiles motivated me to find out more about how they were able to come home with so many health and beauty products for pennies on the dollar, if not completely free, and food at rock bottom prices. I saw there was a pattern to couponing, a system where different women would win at this game....over and over again.

I just needed to learn the formula, the system for success, and implement it.   Since I had hired myself in this new role as "Family Couponer", I knew that there needed to be a time frame for on-the-job-training; so I gave it 30 days. If I were leaving the house to work part-time, I would be gone roughly 15-20 hours a week, so in my mind, I needed to find that time in my weekly schedule and use those hours in training.   I was going to learn all I could possibly learn from others who had gone before me in those 30 days and track all my spending and see if it paid me back in savings.

"Employ your time in improving yourself by other men's writings, so that you shall gain easily what others have labored hard for."
       ~Socrates

By researching strategies and gathering the advice of other successful couponing moms, I found out what I needed to do to be successful. I figured, if we were spending $1600 a month on food, and I could save just 50%, that would be an entire mortgage payment! The challenge was put before me and I was now in the game. The truth of it is, we did save thousands that year. There were months when I would come home with receipts showing 95% savings. We saved so much that year we were able to pay off more debt than we could have ever dreamed possible. Friends wanted to know more, strangers would stop me in the stores, my kids were happy beyond belief at the growing stockpile of goodies in the home.

God was blessing our efforts and they paid off in big ways for our family. Then, as some of you may have experienced, I eventually fell off the coupon clipping train when I became pregnant and in my ninth month. Getting in and out of the car and visiting my several stores was more and more difficult. My family supported me and we lived off our stockpile while we enjoyed our newest baby blessing. The problem was that once I had lost momentum it was really hard to get it back, to push that boulder back uphill.

 With a toddler and a newborn to juggle, getting back on the wagon took a little more time than I had hoped. When money once again became extremely tight, due to an unpredictable market, it became a family necessity for us to jump back into the coupon world full force.

Soon enough, with the help of my kids, we started anew in November of 2010 with our couponing adventures…. in search of quality shampoo at dollar store prices, and an abundance of **name-brand cereal** at no more than **one-dollar-per-box**!

Without fail, the internal voices would discourage me and say, "You've been there and done that and there are only so many tubes of **free toothpaste** one can stand to live with!" I encourage and challenge you, don't listen to those voices! Don't give up! You CAN do this. We'll do this together! It is worth the effort.

"First, have a definite, clear practical ideal; a goal, an objective. Second, have the necessary means to achieve your ends; wisdom, money, materials, and methods. Third, adjust all your means to that end."
    ~Aristotle

If Kroger was a best friend, last summer I broke up with her. She really rocked my world when the Houston area locations all stopped doubling and tripling coupons. In fact, I put this book project in the trash when that rule went into effect because I just knew it was going to be impossible for us to enjoy the same savings we were used to. Then my good friend, Terri Bonin, reminded me why I named this book *The Classical Couponer* in the first place. She told me that BECAUSE our world is changing so fast, with iPhone apps, internet coupons, new extreme coupon TV shows, loyalty card coupons, and ever-changing store policies, the timeless principles of truth, goodness, beauty, and love can (and should) be our motivating force to live within our means today.

As wives and mothers we should continually seek new and better ways to be frugal with our family dollar and teach our children good economic principles.   I do still visit my "friend", Kroger, occasionally to shop strategically, some weeks it may take a little more work, but the savings are available. My favorite sales are when the Kroger Mega Sale cycles back around, you can really see the savings mount up by stockpiling when prices are at their rock-bottom.

One valuable principle worth capturing, is that the work of cutting your grocery bill will be a ***gift to your husband and children***.

Showing your husband that you value his hard work by treating the family income with care is a tremendous blessing to him. For your children, you are teaching them to live below their means and that spending time investing in learning this trade ***is profitable***.

I believe that once you understand the steps to savings, they will become a part of your everyday life. It is awkward in the beginning because you are learning a new skill. I encourage you not to give up, because within just a few weeks you will see the results of your hard work and perseverance.

"Make it your ambition to lead a quiet life and attend to your own business and work with your hands, just as you were instructed." 1 Thess. 4: 11

Get Ready....

THE FIRST WEEK

You're HIRED! Congratulations! You just found a new part-time job. As with all jobs, you need training. There is a learning curve. Commit to spend at least 30 minutes every day studying and learning about couponing and recording your progress. Give yourself 30 days to comprehensively learn this new job and I guarantee you will see the cash rewards.

In order to succeed at something, I am a firm believer in learning how to do things right by imitating what successful people do. As a right-brained learner, visual aids inspire me the most. I recommend one of two things to help you envision wild success as you are gearing up for this new endeavor.

1. Search locally online, or ask your friends for referrals then make an appointment with an experienced couponer in your area and go to his or her home and let them tell you, up close and personal, ***how they save money***. This is

not meant to confuse you with different approaches, but to *inspire* you with someone else's success story. It is true that we tend to move on *emotion* rather than on *reason*. Ask them what they like about couponing, what bothers them, which stores are the friendliest to couponers, and their advice to beginners. You can also join our group on Facebook : *Classical Couponers*.

OR...

2. If you find yourself in the middle of no-man's land, you can go online to one of the many couponing forums. I recommend Terri's message board from **www.thegrocerygame.com** . Type in "stockpiling pictures" or "pantry investment pictures" and you will be motivated! Remember, *we are moved on emotion*! Set your timer to 30 minutes, and read some success stories. Don't get too hung up at first on all the discussion threads, you will have time later, as you work the plan, to read those and learn. We are going to treat the discussion threads as part of your on the job training later.

TIP!! Stop by your local grocery store on a Saturday morning, usually after 10am, and pick up three separate EARLY EDITION SUNDAY papers.

Tip!! *Find out which day of the week the new grocery store sales circulars come to your mailbox and DO NOT THROW THEM OUT! Keep them till they expire, even the stores you will NEVER shop at. These will go in your binder for when you price match at WalMart.*

During your first few days on the job, take some focused time to get a clear picture of how much you spend every month on groceries. Look at your bank statements, check your purse for receipts, or if you are brave…ask your husband. It is essential to know where you are in the beginning with your grocery spending to see the savings at the end of 30 days, and to **know how much your new job is paying you each week.**

Think of it like starting a new weight loss program. You are told to measure yourself and weigh yourself so you can **track your progress**. I cannot overemphasize how important it is to track your spending. Find out what you normally spend, WRITE IT DOWN! This information will be place in your coupon binder as your record of spending. The binder method is explained more in detail below.

FINALLY ~ Ditch the Debit card! Take a trip to the ATM, take out the amount of cash you would **normally** spend in one week (be honest) and stick the CASH in an envelope marked:

GROCERY MONEY FOR THE WEEK OF
_____.

TIP! One of my favorite bloggers is named Tiffany Ivanosky. I like her because her name is like mine ☐, she has lots of kids, and her blog is about ONE DEAL AT A TIME. www.mylitter.com. I LOVE her approach because anyone can do one deal at a time. Each little success will build on the next. Take it slow!

Get Set...

Setting up your system

Here are a few tools you will need to help you get off to a great start:

- Stapler – make sure it works well and you have extra staples.
- Sharp scissors. Eventually you will need a few extra smaller scissors for your future employees 'a.k.a. the kids', but on day one remember that you are working solo.
- Sharpie marker
- Accordion file folder
- Binder - 3-ring, 3-inch zipper binder like you will find at Wal-Mart, or any office supply store. It is essential that you use a zipper binder to protect your coupon stash in case it topples over.
- Bright colored dividers with pockets in them.
- Small calculator
- One standard sized envelope for your grocery cash and store receipts.
- Grocery store sales circulars. Make this a weekly habit to KEEP them when current and PURGE them when expired. They will be

money in your pocket. Our circulars come to my mailbox every Wednesday so I make sure that I get them and put them immediately in my binder if I don't have time to skim them first. We keep the circulars for all the stores so we can use them for our price-matching at WalMart.

Optional:
- Label maker
- Reading glasses (for those of us over 40 visually challenged to read the fine print)
- Computer printer with extra ink and paper for printing online coupons.

Go!!!

Step One: Clear the decks! Set aside a block of time to get started. Saturday mornings work well if you are just beginning. Start with a 4 hour time block then clear a wide space either on the floor or on a table where you can leave your stuff and not have to relocate everything when your time is up.

Turn off your cell phone, unplug your home phone, move the irritating pile of laundry out of sight, send your kids to the neighbors, or let Dad have a park day with them. Don't worry, you will be employing your kids soon enough, but for starters work alone and try to work uninterrupted. My experience has taught me that if we can manage the interruptions ahead of time, we will work more efficiently and productively, which in turn keeps us motivated.

While you are figuring out the couponing system, keeping your head clear is a very *important* factor. Mom needs to figure this system out before she brings in her helpers. Whatever you need to do to clear the decks and your mind so you can begin…do that.

Step Two: Setting up your filing system – There are two approaches you can use with your coupons: Filing by inserts, or the binder method.

I recommend that beginners use the filing by inserts method to start. This is how you will use your accordion file. I actually use a combination of both methods to manage coupons. For your first week on the job, all you need to do is to write on the front of your coupon insert the date and if it is a Smart Source, P&G (Proctor and Gamble), or Red Plum insert. You will write RP 10/23 on the Red Plum insert in the Oct. 23rd edition of the Sunday paper. Or you may write SS 9/17 on the Smart Source Sept 17th edition. This is very important when you begin step FIVE and are hunting for your coupons from the list.

The BINDER has become an essential for many avid couponers. There are several ways to use your binder and it may evolve over time to best fit your style. Youtube has many videos on "how to organize your coupon binder".

 For this first month, I suggest you use the set of bright colored dividers with the pockets in them, and label each divider by stores where you may plan to shop. This is not meant to overwhelm you, but it is part of your systematic approach to couponing and you will add to your system each week.

You are learning a new trade, and this is your grace month. Many couponers have very extraordinary binders with dozens of categories in which to file coupons. You can build that up later, or if you are really eager you can organize your binder in one of three ways:

1. According to your grocery store layout – Recommended if you shop at only one store!

2. A to Z by manufacturer; e.g. "A is for Aquafresh, B is for Betty Crocker, C is for Carmex, etc.

3. By categories. I have found that there is a wide spectrum of categories you can file in your binder. Most of these tend to follow the layout of the grocery store. Since I shop several different stores, I organize my binder with the following categories.

   Examples of categories: Baby, Baking, Beverages, Breads, Breakfast, Canned Goods, Condiments, Dairy/Refrigerated, Frozen Foods, Fresh Foods, General Grocery, Snacks, Pet, Paper Products, Laundry, Cleaning Supplies, Oral Care, Make-up, Feminine Hygiene, Hair Care, Soaps, Other personal care, OTC Medications, Other.

Keep it manageable in the beginning, then you can expand your binder to sub-categories as you become more savvy.

MYTH! You need a coupon for most all the items on your list. FACT! If you print off lists from coupon sites, you will not need to use coupons for every item on your list to save money. Most online deals list the sale prices, any buy one get one free deals, and rock bottom prices. On average my family's lists only have about 15-20% of the items needing a coupon!

Due to the high volume of coupons available each week, it is helpful to also divide into sub-categories for ease of use.

For example:

Sub-Categories

Baby
Diapers
Food
Formula
Medical
Washes and Shampoo
Wipes
Other

Baking
Brownies
Cakes
Cookies
Flour
Gelatin
Mixes
Pudding
Spices
Sugar
Other

Beverages
Coffee
Drink Boxes
Hot Chocolate
Juice
Powdered Mixes
Soda
Tea
Water
Other

Breads
Bagels
Dinner Bread
Dinner Rolls
Donuts
English Muffins
Hamburger Buns
Hot Dog Buns
Pita
Sandwich Bread
Other

Breakfast
Bars
Cereals
Hot Cereals
Oatmeal
Pancake Mix
Syrup
Toaster Pastries
Other

Canned Goods
Beans
Broth
Chilies
Fruits
Meats
Tomatoes
Tuna
Soup- Condensed
Soup- Ready to Eat
Spaghetti Sauce
Vegetables
Other

Condiments
BBQ Sauce
Jelly
Ketchup
Mayonnaise
Mustard
Olives
Peanut Butter
Pickles
Salad Dressing
Sauce/Marinades
Vinegars
Other

Dairy/Refrigerated
Biscuits
Butter/Margarine
Cheese
Cream Cheese
Eggs
Milk
Organic Dairy
Refrigerated Cookie Dough
Yogurt
Other

Frozen Foods
Desserts (cake, pie)
Entrees and Pot Pies
Fish/Seafood
Fruits
Ice Cream & Novelties
Meats
Pizza
Snack Items
TV Dinners
Vegetables
Other

Fresh Foods
Dried Fruits
Meats
Produce
Other

General Grocery
Crackers
Dinner Kits/Entrees
Pasta
Rice
Side Dishes
Stuffing
Other

Snacks
Candy
Cookies
Chips and Pretzels
Nuts/Jerky
Popcorn
Other

Pet
Cat Food
Cat Litter
Dog Food
Treats
Other

Paper Products
Aluminum Foil
Batteries
Paper Napkins
Paper Plates
Paper Towels
Plastic Wrap
Sandwich Baggies
Tissues, Kleenex
Toilet Paper
Wet Wipes
Other

Laundry
Bleach or Whiteners
Dryer Sheets
Fabric Softener
Laundry Soap
Stain Pens
Stain Treatments
Other

Cleaning Supplies
Air Fresheners
All Purpose Cleaner
Bathroom Cleaner
Candles
Dish Soap
Dishwasher Soap
Floor Cleaner
Glass Care
Other

Oral Care
Dental Floss
Mouthwash
Toothbrushes
Toothpastes
Whiteners
Other

Makeup
Almay
Clairol
Cleansers and Makeup
Removers
Cover Girl
Max Factor
Revlon
Tools like Tweezers
Other

Feminine Hygiene
Alternative Products
Cleansers
Maxi Pads
Panty-liners
Tampons
Other

Hair Care
Conditioner

Hair Color
Leave in Treatments
Shampoo

Style Aids
Other

Soaps
Bar Soaps
Body Washes
Hand Soaps
Other
Other Personal Care
Deodorants
Lotions
Razors
Shaving Cream
Other

OTC Medications
Band-aids/First Aid
Cold/Flu
Cough Drops
General
Pain Relievers
Vitamins
Other

Other
Free Product
Entertainment
Rebates
Restaurants
Store coupons

TIP! If you have each store's sales circular with you in the binder, then when you make a quick Wal-*Mart* trip you can price match the lowest prices that week all at one store. Check the blog **www.iheartthemart.com** for weekly price-matching scenarios!

However you choose to organize your coupons in the beginning, either filing by inserts, or with a binder, it is important that you see **SUCCESS** the first week so *keep it simple*. After several years trying different filing techniques, my binder currently has 5 dividers in the front.

With my label maker I have a divider for Kroger, Randalls, HEB, Walmart, CVS, and Target. Then I keep sales circulars in each corresponding divider, along with the store's current coupon policy.

After I have printed off my shopping list from either The Grocery Game website, or the Coupon Mom website, then I put the coupons I've pulled out for each store in the pocket of the divider so I know what I'm looking for if I have to make a quick trip. If your coupons are already filed in your binder, then you may not even want to pull them out until you get to the store.

A well-organized binder is the KEY to couponing success. It is WORTH the time investment to organize it.

Step Three: Gather coupons

The Sunday papers with the weekly inserts will be your first coupons to use. On most Holiday weekends there are generally not any coupon inserts – so double check. I always grab my Sunday papers on Saturday because it gives me a head start on so many deals on the shelves and I don't like to spend my Sundays grocery shopping, (though sometimes it ends up being the best day to shop because of one-day sales).

I recommend **starting small** with just **three papers** is so you can multiply your savings. If you have a large family like I do, you may LATER want to buy one paper per family member; but if you are new to this, buy only three to begin. There are other ways to get coupons, printing online, and mail order services….but for the first week, just get the Sunday papers. Borrow from a friend or family member if you can't buy them, just get them.

Keep your system simple and streamlined as you gather coupons. My reason for this is that I want you to see immediate SUCCESS this first month. As you build up your skills you will find lots of different places to locate coupons.

When I was first married I used to spend HOURS cutting and sorting so many different coupons, I never felt like it was worth all the effort. Then, after several kids came along and I got smarter with my work I learned how to clip coupons from TEN different newspapers in just under an HOUR!

Take each insert and lay them out separately on the floor or a table. Grab the first page of each insert and staple the pages together. Be sure not to staple over the bar code. After you have stapled all the inserts, then cut the coupons in stacks based on how many papers you purchased, and file into your system.

Step Four: <u>Hit the computer!</u>

Not literally, but with laser focus and control. The coupon world online has literally exploded in the past 5 years. Online lists of shopping deals are a modern busy woman's BEST FRIEND. They are equivalent to other time-saving inventions such as refrigerators, washing machines, and indoor plumbing! These lists will save you time as well as money.

At first it can be very overwhelming. I'm a veteran and still find it a challenge to maneuver through all the websites, however, it is well worth it. There is no need for you to re-invent the wheel when it comes to saving money.

There are other moms in different parts of the country that have awakened VERY EARLY to check ALL the good deals for US to enjoy. Use this resource, it will pay you back. I will tell you that nothing is 100% accurate due to slight variations nationwide; however, you will still save money by printing off a list from the top coupon websites. My two favorites are: **www.thegrocerygame.com** and **www.couponmom.com** .

Sign up for either one. The Coupon Mom site is free to join, and the grocery game has a minimal charge that is well worth it. I use both.

You will need to print your list by choosing the stores where you shop. Also print off a copy of your store's coupon policy. Check the website for a list of stores in your state and all of the coupon policies.

Put these print outs in your binder. Later, you can get into the habit of loading e-coupons to your store loyalty card. Eventually you will be printing some of your favorite and most frequently used coupons online. Take a few minutes to sign up with your email on the grocery store websites. They will mail you special promotions and send the weekly flyers to your inbox.

After the first couple of weeks when you are feeling your first wave of successes, I encourage you to sign up for other email newsletters to come right to your inbox. Ask your tech-savvy hubby or teen how to direct these emails to their own individual folder so as not to fill up your inbox. These are great, quick resources you can use weekly to scan the best deals and pick one or two that jump out at you. Some great blogs whose newsletters I have delivered to my inbox are included at the end of this section.

Step Five: Clip or Pull your coupons.

Your list will tell you which coupons to clip. As previously mentioned, there are two approaches to coupon clipping. The first is to save your inserts and put the date on the front with a sharpie marker, then file in your accordion file until you need them. The other is to clip everything and file the clipped coupons in your binder. THIS IS THE STEP that will OVERWHELM YOU. Do not quit here! **Success is near**.

The reason I think that we get paralyzed on this step is because of the sheer volume of coupons. **Just pull out the ones from the list to the store where you are going to shop, and put them in your binder pocket dividers, one for each store**. Or you can put the store specific coupons in an envelope with the name of the store on the front.

Step Six: <u>Shop!</u>

For the first few times as you are getting started, I highly recommend *shopping alone*. Do not shop when you are exhausted or hungry. Let your family know that this is mommy's new job and *you need to be at peak performance to maximize your savings.*

Bring your list in your binder that you have printed off from your favorite coupon site along with all the matching coupons you pulled.

As you pick up something from your list, slip the coupon you will use at the checkout into a separate section so you can grab them all at once at checkout.

People often ask me when the best day and time to shop is. That will depend on several factors. We love shopping at our mega grocery store on the weekends (or the busiest days) because they have more checkers working and they give out lots of free samples; which can also come with high dollar coupons.

I've found over the years that if I shop at night when I *think* no one is there, it actually takes me much longer to check out because there are fewer checkers and often very cranky managers on duty.

Tip! *TEACH YOUR KIDS that NO ONE talks to Mom at the checkout!* *Habit: Turn off your cell phone at the checkout counter or give it to your oldest child.* *Distractions will cost you money when shopping this way. Pay attention to **every scanned item.***

Shopping earlier in the day, before noon, seems to be the best time of day for markdowns in the meat departments. If I shop later in the day, most of those bargains are gone. Butchers seem to work earlier in the day and will rotate meat out at that time. Learn your own grocery store's patterns and shop accordingly.

Get on first name basis with the managers in the Dairy, Bakery, Meat, and Produce departments. They are often more than happy to let you in on some great deals and when they will mark down items in their department. Be sure to thank them with a good tip of your own.

For example: Once a year our local Chick-fil-A gives away free meals to anyone who comes into their restaurant dressed like a cow. It's called "Cow Appreciation Day". Our family takes Dad's old white t-shirts and a sharpie marker and we make cow shirts and paint our faces and go into Chick-fil-A for either a free breakfast, lunch, or dinner.

As my thank you to my favorite store managers, I made sure I stopped into the store that day and told them how they could get a free lunch or dinner across the street. We were pretty much a spectacle walking through the store, me and all the kids in cow faces, but the managers really appreciated it.

Step Seven: <u>Track your savings</u>.

Use cash for all your transactions when shopping with coupons. This is a habit that ***will pay you back ten-fold*** later on as you build up your skill set. There are certain drugstore deals that will come up as you build your experience where you can get up to 90% savings and literally pay pennies at the checkout. If you are in the habit of keeping a grocery cash envelope, then you will be ready when those smaller transactions happen. Also, if you have a certain weekly shopping budget you are used to; keep that amount at the beginning of your new job.

The money left in your envelope at the end of the week…

.<u>**IS YOUR PAYCHECK** ☺</u>.

"A penny saved is a penny earned"
~Benjamin Franklin

After you have double-checked your receipts, place all your receipts together in an envelope and write on the outside your savings when you get home from the store. The outsides of my envelopes have three columns: Amount Spent, Amount Saved (you'll see this at the bottom of your receipt), and Shelf Value (those two numbers added together).

Tracking these savings will be another tool in your tool belt that helps to motivate you to keep on going. For those of you who are the high-tech moms, you can track your weekly savings on a simple spreadsheet or on your iPhones.

Step Eight: <u>Sharpen your skills</u>

"Always desire to learn something useful"
~**Sophocles**

Have you ever felt like you work so hard for such little results when it comes to trying to save money with coupons? Stephen R. Covey illustrates,

Suppose you were to come upon someone in the woods

working feverishly to saw down a tree.

"What are you doing?" you ask.

"Can't you see?" comes the impatient reply. *"I'm sawing down this tree."*

"You look exhausted!" you exclaim. *"How long have you been at it?"*

"Over five hours," he returns, *"and I'm beat! This is hard work."*

'Well, why don't you take a break for a few minutes and sharpen that saw?" you inquire. *"I'm sure it would go a lot faster."*

"I don't have time to sharpen the saw," the man says emphatically. *"I'm too busy sawing!"*

"If the ax is dull and its edge unsharpened, more strength is needed but skill will bring success." **Eccl 10:10**

It is my hope and desire that as you begin your new job as Professional Family Couponer, you will **work smarter and not harder**. Step Eight will help you be more effective in your work.

How do you sharpen your skills? Besides your weekly routine of gather, clip, sort, shop, and review, a few times during your week: read the online coupon forums, follow the threads, ask questions, spend a couple of hours just reading over the new websites you discover. Track what you are learning in a journal or notebook. Your goal is going to be small, measurable successes. Let each success build upon the next one. It is better to build your business at a slow and steady rate, than to try reaching the unrealistic goal of 'extreme couponer' status the first week!

You want beauty, balance, blessing, and bounty in your home as a result of your new job. A good rule of thumb is to use the low energy downtimes of your week to sharpen your skills at couponing. You can look on youtube.com for "ways to organize coupons" and find several different techniques and methods from experienced shoppers.

There are also helpful resources to teach you "how to use coupons at the drugstores". Use these times to keep your mind sharp and learn new tips and tricks each week. My husband is a huge baseball fan, so I like to sit on the couch with my laptop while he's watching sports and I will just look over different tips online.

"An investment in knowledge pays the best interest."
~Benjamin Franklin

Step Nine: <u>Hire your kids!</u>

After you have gone through the weekly process, and when you feel a little more confident, you can add more employees to your team. After awhile, our family gets into a rhythm with couponing. We purchase our newspapers Saturday morning, then I usually have two or three helpers to stack, staple, clip, and sort our coupons into piles.

A great rule of thumb is: Mom does what only SHE can do, and she delegates the rest to the kids. The brain work and the shopping needs to be mom's job, but you can outsource all the clipping, sorting, loading and unloading groceries, pantry organization, and even some meal planning and cooking to your kids.However, if I have my kids clipping everything and not just filing by inserts, it is important for me to be able to glance over all the clipped piles of coupons at least once in order to know what we have. I have learned that if I don't look at the coupons, but let my kids do all the clipping and filing, I miss out on some deals because my brain won't have triggered that we had a particular coupon.

After your first week of shopping, when you begin to see your savings in real dollars from your cash envelope *that still has cash in it*, you can pay your kids out of that savings. I am not a mom who overpays her kids. I want them to understand the value of every dollar! While they are young, I am amazed at how much they will do for the family (with a happy heart) if I just let them pick out one thing at the Dollar Store!

Remember, your kids are benefitting with all the extra food and household items you will be stockpiling in your home. They will also greatly benefit as they see mom and dad able to give away so much from the family's abundant stockpile in times of crises. Keeping a large stockpile is a great way to bless your neighbors, and community with the abundance in your pantry.

"All the gold which is under or upon the earth is not enough to give in exchange for virtue. "
~Plato

As a homeschooling mom of eight kids all ages, I'm always looking for activities for the kids to do that will add value to our home and our family. I believe that our kids are our biggest untapped resources and they are capable of much more than we expect. Recently, my son, Benjamin, began a new project completely on his own.

I am not sure how this project started, but he decided to start calling companies of his favorite food products. He looked up the customer service number on the websites of companies like Jif®, Tostitos®, Dr. Pepper®, Johnsonville Sausage®, Pillsbury®, and so on. His conversation sounded like this…

"Hi! My name is Ben Lichnovsky. I'm 12 years old. I am calling you to let you know that our family really loves your 'Pillsbury Cinnamon Rolls'. In fact, when we eat them, it takes THREE whole packages just to feed our family of TEN. I wanted you to know you were all doing a good job and to keep it up!"

The customer service representative would then ask him if a parent was nearby to which he would respond 'YES'. The next thing I would hear from Ben was, "Coupons? Oh, we would LOVE you to send us some coupons!" Then, Ben would track each call on a spreadsheet whether or not he contacted them by email, their website, phone, or snail mail. He tracked how they responded, and what they offered to send him (if anything), and how long it took before arriving in the mail or to his inbox.

After several hours, he had a long list of companies he had contacted. This marketing research was fun for him AND mom as fun surprises began arriving in the mail.   Sometimes he received a high-value coupon for a free item, other times it was a recipe.

The point is, he was spending time on something that was benefitting our family.   Not only can a coupon hobby eventually pay you a salary, but also when you employ your children in the process the benefits increase exponentially. Twelve year old Ben writes:

Ever since my Mom started couponing, we ALL have been happier. We get more food because we save more money. We never really got the healthy name brand cereals until my Mom started couponing…then one day we came home from shopping and we stacked all the cereal boxes up and they were taller than me! I am my mom's assistant whenever she goes out shopping. There are many benefits to being an assistant. For example,

- Sometimes I walk around the store with my baby sister in her stroller, and try all of the free samples ☺.
- I get a workout by pushing around the cart that is filled up to the top whenever it gets too heavy for Mom.
- I learned that I could get a whole lot more with a dollar than just ONE bottle of Dr. Pepper.
- I get to listen in on my Mom's 'discussions' with the store managers about the sale policy. Sometimes they get pretty exciting.

Step TEN – <u>Repeat steps 3-7 weekly</u>

*"Excellence is an art won by training and habituation. We do not act rightly because we have virtue or excellence, but we rather have those because we have acted rightly. We are what we repeatedly do. Excellence, then, is not an act but a habit." ~**Aristotle***

We learn through repetition, these steps are simple and easy to follow so you will experience winning results immediately. Share them with a friend and teach them to your kids.

In conclusion, it is my hope and prayer that you find great success with your couponing plan and that God will bless your industry and your hard work as your glorify Him in all things….even saving money ☺.

Some additional helpful information:
Where else can I get coupons?

1. Sunday Newspapers
2. Printable Sites
3. Manufacturers Websites
4. In-Store
5. In the Mail
6. Magazines
7. E-Coupons or Loadable coupons
8. Coupon Clipping Sites

What do all those letters mean online?   *Learn the Lingo!*

WYB = When You Buy

BOGO or BOGOF = Buy One Get One Free

FAR = Free After Rebate

IP = Internet Printable Coupon

IVC = Instant Value Coupon at Walgreens (Walgreens store coupon).

MIR = Mail In Rebate

OYNO = On Your Next Order

OOP = Out of Pocket.

RP = Red Plum insert

SS = SmartSource insert

P&G = Procter and Gamble insert

GM = General Mills insert (usually a SmartSource insert)

Moneymaker: Getting something better than free after coupons and sale.

CAT = Catalina coupon that prints at check out.

YMMV = Your Mileage May Vary. It can also mean: Your manager may vary. Everyone may have a different experience

ECB = Extra Care Buck (CVS coupon good on your next order)

RR = Register Rewards (Walgreens Rewards program, Manufacturer coupon good on your next order)

SCR = Single Check Rebate (Rite Aid rebate program)

Helpful websites

www.couponmom.com

www.thegrocerygame.com

www.couponcoach.com

www.mylitter.com

www.savingwithamy.com

www.dealseekingmom.com

www.forthemommas.com

www.wickedcooldeals.com

www.wildforwags.com

www.iheartkroger.com

www.iheartthemart.com

www.totallytarget.com

www.shortcuts.com

www.weusecoupons.com

www.frugallivingandhavingfun.com

www.smartcouponing.com

www.commonsensewithmoney.com

www.freecouponalerts.com